"We join together this season, bound together by love, joy, and commitment. Like the lion, like the eagle, like the elephant — we are powerful and strong. Like the sky, like the ocean, like the forests — we are forever. Kwanzaa is our time to remember and to continue."

— A KWANZAA LIBATION

KWANZAA

By Amy Robin Jones

The Child's World®

GRAPHIC DESIGN
Robert E. Bonaker / Graphic Design & Consulting Co.

PROJECT COORDINATOR
James R. Rothaus / James R. Rothaus & Associates

EDITORIAL DIRECTION
Elizabeth Sirimarco Budd

COVER PHOTO
A Kwanzaa Setting
©David M. Budd Photography

With gratitude for the help of Limbiko Tembo
and the University of Sankore Press.

Library of Congress Cataloging-in-Publication Data
Jones, Amy Robin, 1958–
Kwanzaa / by Amy Robin Jones.
p. cm.
Includes bibliographical references and index.
Summary: Describes the origin and meaning of the African
American holiday which has been celebrated each year
since 1966 from December 26 to January 1.
ISBN 1-56766-719-8 (lib. reinforced : alk. paper)

1. Kwanzaa — Juvenile literature. 2. Afro-Americans — Social
life and customs — Juvenile literature. [1. Kwanzaa. 2. Afro-
Americans — Social life and customs. 3. Holidays.] I. Title

GT4403 .J68 2000
394.261 — dc21   99-048445

Contents

What Is Kwanzaa?

When winter is at its peak and spring and summer seem far away, many people take time to celebrate both seasonal and religious holidays. The Jewish holiday is known as Chanukah (HAH-nuh-kuh). The Christian celebration is Christmas. Muslims observe a holiday called Ramadan (RAW-meh-dahn). A special time for African Americans is Kwanzaa (pronounced KWAHN-zah). Kwanzaa is a holiday that celebrates family, community, and **culture.** Unlike Christmas, Chanukah, and Ramadan, Kwanzaa is not a religious holiday.

During Kwanzaa, African Americans remember the traditions and history of their **ancestors.** They honor people and events. Kwanzaa reminds African Americans to celebrate who they are. It also gives them **principles** by which to live.

How did Kwanzaa come to be? An **activist** and teacher named Dr. Maulana Karenga created this holiday in 1966. (Dr. Karenga's name is pronounced mah-oo-LAH-nah kah-RAYN-gah.) He realized that many African Americans wanted to learn more about their **heritage.** Their ancestors came from the continent of Africa, where people had their own special **customs,** languages, songs, and stories. Dr. Karenga believed African Americans needed a special time to honor their own culture, so he created Kwanzaa.

This holiday is also an opportunity for African American families to gather together. It is an opportunity for them to celebrate who they are and all their accomplishments of the past year. They can celebrate and say "thank you," (*"asante,"*) for the good things that have happened. They also make plans for the year to come.

Julie Bidwell/Stock, Boston

KWANZAA IS A CELEBRATION THAT HONORS AFRICAN HERITAGE. ABOUT 13 MILLION AFRICAN AMERICANS CELEBRATE KWANZAA EACH YEAR. PEOPLE IN OTHER PARTS OF THE WORLD CELEBRATE KWANZAA, TOO.

The word Kwanzaa comes from the **Swahili** language, as do the words that describe the traditions and symbols of the holiday. *Matunda ya kwanzaa* means "first fruits." First fruits come from the **harvest.** People all over the world celebrate when they harvest fruits and vegetables. Kwanzaa is based on African winter harvest celebrations. It is a time to be together. It is a time to honor creation. It is a time to remember family members who came before us (our ancestors) and to remember what we have done during the past year. It is a time to **commit** ourselves to principles that improve our lives. It is a time to celebrate for the good things in our lives.

During Kwanzaa, we can think of our accomplishments and the good things in our lives as something we have "harvested." Perhaps you have a new member of the family or have earned good grades. Someone else may have learned to play the piano or a sport. Some girls and boys collect food and clothes for the homeless. Others volunteer at a retirement home, an animal shelter, or their church. Kwanzaa is a time to remember, to look back at all we have accomplished. It is a time to look at all the good things in our lives and to think about what we want to do in the future.

Swahili Pronunciation

The following guide will help you pronounce the Swahili words that describe Kwanzaa traditions. The glossary on page 38 includes more information about how to say the Swahili words in this book.

a = ah, as in father
e = a, as in day
i = ee, as in free
o = o, as in go
u = oo, as in too

Courtesy of Dr. Maulana Karenga, Black Studies Department, California State University, Long Beach

DR. KARENGA CREATED KWANZAA IN 1966. AT THE TIME, HE WAS A STUDENT AND THE HEAD OF A GROUP CALLED US. THIS ORGANIZATION WAS COMMITTED TO LEARNING ABOUT AFRICAN HISTORY AND THEN TEACHING IT TO AFRICAN AMERICANS. AFTER CREATING KWANZAA, KARENGA AND OTHER MEMBERS OF US TRAVELED AROUND THE COUNTRY TO TELL PEOPLE ABOUT IT.

The Seven Principles: The Nguzo Saba

Kwanzaa is a holiday that lasts for seven days. The celebration begins on December 26 and ends on January 1. These seven days are to remind people of the central principles of Kwanzaa, called the *Nguzo Saba*. The phrase means "the Seven Principles." These principles represent positive ways for people to live.

Dr. Karenga saw that many African Americans were working together to make their communities better. Many organizations were started to improve the lives of African Americans, too. To help people remember this **commitment,** Dr. Karenga developed Seven Principles, or seven rules, for living. He said these principles were ways that black people must live to build better lives for themselves and their families. Each day of Kwanzaa represents one of these principles. People who celebrate Kwanzaa think about the principle for that day. The following are the Nguzo Saba.

1. *UMOJA* (unity)

Unity means working together, playing together, living together. It is a feeling of community shared with family, friends, people at school, and especially with the community of African Americans. In Africa, there is a saying: "I am because we are. And because we are, therefore I am."

2. *KUJICHAGULIA* (self-determination)

If you make up your own mind to do something, and to do it as best you can, then you have self-determination. You need self-determination for many things: to study, to work, and to get along with other people. You make decisions because you know they are the best ones for you, your family, and the community.

Lawrence Migdale/Stock, Boston

On each day of Kwanzaa, people gather to celebrate one of the Nguzo Saba. You can celebrate Kwanzaa with your family, friends, classmates, and neighbors.

3. *UJIMA* (collective work or "working together" and responsibility)
People should work together to build family, community, and the world. Share the problems and goals of those around you. Working together solves problems and builds communities. We all have a responsibility to help others.

4. *UJAMAA* (sharing — Dr. Karenga calls this "cooperative economics")
Share what you have with your community, and support your community. The more you share, the more everybody has!

5. *NIA* (purpose)
African tradition says that our main purpose in life is to bring good into the world. If you do good things, your life has purpose.

6. *KUUMBA* (creativity)
Think of how you like to express yourself. How could you tell other people something about you? Could you do it with a poem, a dance, or a picture? Being creative is part of sharing yourself with friends and family.

7. *IMANI* (faith)
Having faith means to believe in yourself and your abilities. It also means to believe and trust in your parents, your teachers, and in leaders who help to make the world a better place.

KWANZAA

33 USA

1999

©David M. Budd Photography

In 1997 and 1999, the U.S. Postal Service released special stamps in honor of Kwanzaa. Dr. Karenga said this recognized "the importance of Kwanzaa to African people throughout the world." It also showed how the United States can respect and celebrate its many peoples and cultures.

How We Celebrate Kwanzaa

Kwanzaa begins on December 26. This is Umoja, the first day of Kwanzaa. People call out to each other, *"Habari gani?"* This means "What's the news?" The answer is Umoja, the first principle. Each day of Kwanzaa, the same question is asked: Habari gani? The answer is always the principle of that day.

If you go into a home where Kwanzaa is celebrated, you'll find different symbols that have special meanings, just as the Nguzo Saba, the Seven Principles, do. Two important symbols are the *mishumaa saba* and the *kinara*. The mishumaa saba are candles that represent each of the Seven Principles of Kwanzaa. There are three red candles, three green candles, and one black candle. These are the three colors of Kwanzaa. Black represents black people all around the world. Red represents their struggle. Green represents hope and the future.

The candles are placed in a wooden candleholder called a *kinara*. The kinara represents ancestors. Ancestors are family members that came before us, such as our great-great grandparents. Learning about their lives can teach us how to live. Each day, a candle representing one of the Nguzo Saba is lit. Then everybody talks about that principle and what it means.

The black candle goes in the middle of the kinara. The red candles are placed to the left of the black candle, and the green candles are placed to the right of it. The black candle is the first one lit. This is to symbolize that people are the most important part of the celebration. Each night that follows, another candle is lit, alternating from left to right, until all seven candles are lit together.

THERE ARE MANY SYMBOLS AND SPECIAL OBJECTS THAT ARE PART OF A KWANZAA CELEBRATION. THE KINARA IS A WOODEN CANDLEHOLDER THAT HOLDS SEVEN CANDLES, ONE FOR EACH DAY OF KWANZAA. THE BLACK, RED, AND GREEN CANDLES ARE CALLED THE MISHUMAA SABA. LIGHTING THE CANDLES IS AN IMPORTANT CUSTOM DURING KWANZAA.

©David M. Budd Photography

KWANZAA IS PATTERNED AFTER AFRICAN WINTER HARVEST FESTIVALS. THE MAZAO ARE FRUITS AND VEGETABLES THAT SYMBOLIZE THE CROPS FROM THE FIRST HARVEST OF THE YEAR. THEY ARE PLACED IN AN AFRICAN STRAW BASKET.

Mazao, which means crops, is another important Kwanzaa symbol. The mazao are fruits and vegetables placed in an African straw basket. They symbolize our collective work (working together) and the rewards of our work at the harvest. The *muhindi* are ears of corn that symbolize children.

Families have one muhindi for each child. But even families or groups with no children include at least one muhindi at a Kwanzaa celebration. This is because the muhindi represent children and the African idea of social parenthood. In many African communities, everyone shares the responsibility of raising each child. Everyone in the community helps teach and care for all of the children. Muhindi also represent another idea — that children are the future.

The *mkeka* is another symbol of Kwanzaa. It is a straw mat that symbolizes the history and traditions of African culture. The *kikombe cha umoja* is a wooden cup that symbolizes unity. It is used for a **libation**. A libation is an act of respect to remember and honor ancestors. To perform a libation, the wooden cup is filled. Then the cup is tilted, and some of the liquid is poured onto the ground. People often give a short speech as they perform a libation.

Kwanzaa is celebrated for seven nights by lighting a candle. But some people will join together at larger celebrations and light every candle on a single evening. However it is celebrated, Kwanzaa is a time to be with loved ones. We can let others know how much we love them by giving a *zawadi*, a Kwanzaa gift often made by hand.

©David M. Budd Photography

A special Kwanzaa feast is called the *karamu*, which is celebrated on December 31. Everyone brings food from different parts of the world African community. There are recipes at the end of this book for the karamu.

Every family or group of people can have different things to do during Kwanzaa. Still others enjoy telling African folk tales to each other. Some will read and study. Others will help elders in the community. Many families plan special activities for their neighborhoods to celebrate each day of Kwanzaa. But everyone gathers to light the candles, and everyone thinks about the Nguzo Saba. At the end of the celebration, people will say *"Asante, asante sana,"* which means "Thank you, thank you very much!" and *Tutaonang,* which means "we will see each other again." Then the following night, people come together once more to celebrate. One of the nicest things about Kwanzaa is taking time to spend with friends and family.

THE KIKOMBE CHA UMOJA IS A WOODEN CUP THAT SYMBOLIZES UNITY. IT IS USED FOR THE LIBATION, A TRADITION THAT HONORS AFRICAN ANCESTORS.

ZAWADI ARE KWANZAA GIFTS. WHEN DR. KARENGA CREATED KWANZAA, HE SAID THAT ALL KWANZAA GIFTS SHOULD BE MADE BY HAND. TODAY MANY PEOPLE GIVE BOOKS AND MUSIC BY AFRICAN AMERICANS. OTHERS GIVE AFRICAN CLOTHING AND ART WORK. DR. KARENGA SAYS PEOPLE SHOULD CHOOSE ZAWADI MADE BY AFRICANS AND AFRICAN AMERICANS TO GIVE AT KWANZAA.

The Seven Days of Kwanzaa

Before the beginning of Kwanzaa, people choose a special place in the house to display the symbols of the celebration. First, they place the mkeka where their family can gather together. Usually, people place it on a table covered with beautiful African fabric called *kente.* Then they put the kinara in the center of the mkeka. Next, they place the black, red, and green candles in the kinara. The muhindi are placed on either side of the kinara. Then people place the zawadi (gifts), kikombe cha umoja (unity cup), and a basket of mazao (crops) on the mkeka.

Each day of Kwanzaa has special traditions that make it different from the other six days. Following are the **rituals** for each day.

The first day of Kwanzaa is December 26. The black candle is lit, and people talk about Umoja (unity).

The second day of Kwanzaa is December 27. The black candle is lit, and then the first red candle next to it is lit. There is talk about Kujichagulia (self-determination).

The third day of Kwanzaa is December 28. First, people light the black candle. Then they light the red candle to the left of it and the green candle to the right of it. The principle of the day is Ujima, collective work (working together) and responsibility. Those gathered together talk about how they can work together and be responsible for one another.

AFRICAN AMERICANS CELEBRATE KWANZAA AT HOME, BUT SOMETIMES CLASSMATES WILL SHARE A CELEBRATION AT SCHOOL.

The fourth day of Kwanzaa is December 29. As people begin to light more candles, they must remember to always start in the center and move outward, first to the left, then to the right, and then to the left again. On the fourth night, people light the black candle first, as they do on every night of Kwanzaa. Next, the first red candle to the left of the black candle is lit, followed by the first green candle to the right of it. Finally, the second red candle is lit. Ujamaa (sharing) is the principle of the day, and people think about how they can share all of the "wealth" they have — knowledge, skills, and the ability to be kind, for example.

The fifth day of Kwanzaa is December 30. People light the candles just as they did the night before, adding the second green candle. They discuss Nia (purpose) and what is one's purpose in life.

The sixth day of Kwanzaa is December 31. As always, the black candle is lit first, and then alternating from left to right, three red candles and two green candles are lit. There is talk about Kuumba principle (creativity). The karamu (feast) is held on December 31. Many families enjoy a feast of African foods. They also sing, dance, and play games together. They celebrate the good things in life.

The seventh and last day of Kwanzaa is January 1. All the candles are lit — the black candle, the three red candles, and the three green candles. The principle of Imani (faith) is the most important of the day. There is talk of the people in whom one can have faith: parents, teachers, leaders, relatives, and friends. The last day of Kwanzaa is also the Day of **Meditation.** It is a day to think about one's life and family, about the community, and about the African culture. It is a day to think about how we can make each of these good things even better.

©David M. Budd Photography

A SPECIAL TABLE SETTING THAT INCLUDES THE SYMBOLS OF KWANZAA IS A BIG PART OF THE CELEBRATION.

©David M. Budd Photography

STORYTELLING IS A FAVORITE PART OF A KWANZAA CELEBRATION. CHILDREN GATHER AND LISTEN TO FOLK TALES FROM AFRICA. HERE A STORYTELLER SPRINKLES GRAIN INTO CHILDREN'S HANDS AS SHE REMINDS THEM THAT KWANZAA CELEBRATES THE HARVEST OF CROPS.

Every family or group can create its own special Kwanzaa celebration. Many families like to decorate their homes using the African colors of black, red, and green. They may wear traditional African clothes, too, such as a *kanga* (a brightly colored, loose-fitting garment worn by women) and a *buba* (a long shirt, usually worn by men).

On the first night, the celebration can begin with someone asking the question, "Habari gani?" This means, "What's the news?" Everyone calls back Umoja (unity). After all the guests arrive, someone offers a *kukaribisha* (welcoming). Guests are introduced and welcomed to the family. Songs are sung, stories are told, and poetry is recited. Then people can take turns remembering ancestors or important people. Some people tell stories about their family, such as grandparents, aunts, and uncles. Other celebrations may include stories about important African Americans such as Martin Luther King, Jr., Mary McLeod Bethune, Malcolm X, Rosa Parks, and Marcus Garvey. There are many, many African Americans to remember!

Next, someone may give a short talk about the past year and the year to come. This is called the *kuchunguza tena na kutoa ahadi tena* (**reassessment** and **recommitment**). People can say something about their goals and hopes for the new year.

But most important, the family and guests should rejoice in each other's company. They should celebrate and remember their culture. Together, the gathering of people lights the candles, pours the libation, and remembers ancestors. The whole group thinks about how lucky they are to be together at such a happy time.

Questions About Kwanzaa

CAN YOU STILL CELEBRATE CHRISTMAS? Yes, Kwanzaa is not a substitute for Christmas. It is another holiday that symbolizes different things. But remember that when people celebrate Kwanzaa, they should not combine it with Christmas or other celebrations. It is important to enjoy its traditions separately.

DO YOU HAVE TO BE BLACK TO CELEBRATE KWANZAA? Kwanzaa was created for African American families, but many people who are not black are invited to celebrate. They enjoy participating and learning about the holiday. Anyone can celebrate Kwanzaa, but it would be helpful to know as much as you can about it. Remember that Kwanzaa focuses on being together and appreciating African heritage, not on giving gifts.

©David M. Budd Photography

AT KWANZAA, SOME CHILDREN LEARN TO SING SONGS IN SWAHILI OR ANOTHER AFRICAN LANGUAGE. THEN THEY PERFORM THE SONGS FOR THEIR FAMILIES.

©David M. Budd Photography

PEOPLE WEAR CLOTHING MADE FROM BEAUTIFUL
AFRICAN FABRICS DURING KWANZAA. MUSICIANS
PLAY A BEAT ON TRADITIONAL DRUMS AS OTHER
PEOPLE SING AFRICAN SONGS.

©David M. Budd Photography

KWANZAA USUALLY IS CELEBRATED BY AFRICAN AMERICANS, BUT PEOPLE FROM MANY BACKGROUNDS LIKE TO LEARN ABOUT THIS SPECIAL EVENT. WHEN PEOPLE ORGANIZE CELEBRATIONS AT COMMUNITY CENTERS AND OTHER PLACES, THEY OFTEN INVITE ANYONE WHO IS INTERESTED IN ATTENDING.

WHAT DO THE COLORS OF THE CANDLES MEAN? Black is for black people all around the world, not just in America. Red symbolizes struggle — the hard work that African people have done and will continue to do. Green represents the hope for a better future that comes from struggle.

WHAT IS A GOOD KWANZAA GIFT? The best gifts, or zawadi, at Kwanzaa are like any gift, something that you want to give to others because you care about them. Kwanzaa gifts should have special meaning, though. The zawadi should always include one book and a "heritage symbol," which is something that has to do with African culture. You can give a book about Africa, African Americans, or African history or culture. Other ideas include kente cloth, which has an African design. You could also give people a gift that you made especially for them. The holiday celebrates African family, community, and culture. Keep that in mind when choosing gifts for the people you care about. Most often, zawadi are given to children. Although gifts may be given to adults, this is kept to a minimum. People who celebrate Kwanzaa should try to focus on family, community, and culture instead of giving gifts.

THERE ARE MANY WAYS TO ENJOY KWANZAA. TRY MAKING YOUR OWN MKEKA FOR THE CELEBRATION. YOU CAN USE COLORFUL PAPER INSTEAD OF STRAW.

©Bob Daemmrich/Stock, Boston

Kwanzaa Projects

What are some ways that you can make Kwanzaa special? Try some of these projects!

WRITE ABOUT THE NGUZO SABA. Give examples of what you can do in your home, school, and community to honor each principle. Interview other people (your parents, teachers, brothers, sisters, grandparents, librarians, and others) about how they live their lives according to the Nguzo Saba.

REMEMBER, AFRICA IS A CONTINENT WITH MANY DIFFERENT COUNTRIES. Study a map of Africa and learn the different names and locations of the countries. Learn about different customs in each country. (See page 40 for recommended books on this and other subjects.)

READ AFRICAN FOLK TALES AND AFRICAN AMERICAN STORIES.

LEARN WORDS FROM AN AFRICAN LANGUAGE, SUCH AS SWAHILI.

MAKE LISTS OF AFRICAN AMERICANS WHO HAVE CONTRIBUTED TO THEIR CULTURE. Include in your list scientists, inventors, educators, and leaders. Read their biographies or autobiographies. Some examples include: Marian Anderson, Maya Angelou, Mary McLeod Bethune, George Washington Carver, Frederick Douglass, Marcus Garvey, Fannie Lou Hammer, Barbara Jordan, Maulana Karenga, Coretta Scott King, Martin Luther King, Jr., Toussaint L'Ouverture, Malcolm X, Thurgood Marshall, Toni Morrison, Rosa Parks, Sojourner Truth, and Alice Walker.

©David M. Budd Photography

A FUN KWANZAA PROJECT IS TO PREPARE A PLAY OR DANCE ABOUT AFRICAN CULTURE. THEN YOU CAN PERFORM IT FOR YOUR FAMILY AND FREINDS.

©David M. Budd Photography

STORYTELLERS HELP US REMEMBER AFRICAN AMERICAN FOLK TALES AND HISTORY. LOOK FOR SPECIAL STORIES THAT YOU CAN SHARE WITH FAMILY AND FRIENDS.

PREPARE A GARDEN TO HARVEST FOR NEXT YEAR'S KWANZAA. If you live in a warm climate, prepare a garden to harvest for next year's Kwanzaa. Now is the time to make a list of the plants you would like to grow.

VISIT MUSEUMS OR ART GALLERIES TO LOOK AT AFRICAN ART.

LISTEN TO MUSIC THAT COMES FROM AFRICA OR IS PERFORMED BY AFRICAN AMERICANS. A musical group called *Sweet Honey in the Rock* has a song called "Seven Principles." Study the history of black music in America, including **spirituals,** blues, ragtime, jazz, rock and roll, and rap.

MAKE A COOKBOOK OF YOUR FAMILY'S FAVORITE KWANZAA FOOD. Try to get all your relatives involved. Include grandparents, aunts, uncles, cousins, and more. The book can be a very special zawadi for your friends.

©Lawrence Migdale/Stock, Boston

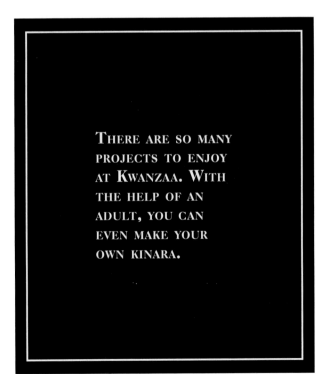

THERE ARE SO MANY PROJECTS TO ENJOY AT KWANZAA. WITH THE HELP OF AN ADULT, YOU CAN EVEN MAKE YOUR OWN KINARA.

Kwanzaa Food

Remember that the colors for Kwanzaa are black, red, and green. You might try to find food in these colors to make a creative dish. Make lists of all the foods you can think of that are these colors.

Some foods that originally came from Africa include pumpkins, sweet potatoes, squash, bananas, mangoes, plantains, and watermelon. Here are some recipes for foods you can make for the karamu. Ask your parents or other adults to help you, especially for recipes that use hot oil or high cooking temperatures.

SOUTH AFRICAN SWEET POTATO FRITTERS

1 pound sweet potatoes
1/2 cup flour
1 egg, beaten
salt and pepper to taste

Heat oil in a saucepan to 375 degrees.

Grate the sweet potatoes and cover them with boiling water. Let them sit for 15 minutes. Drain the water off and add the remaining ingredients, stirring gently. When you have a thick paste, drop the spoonfuls of the mixture into the hot oil and cook the fritters for 3 to 5 minutes, until they float to the surface. Turn the fritters once to make sure they are browned on each side. Drain and serve hot.

CARAMELIZED PLANTAINS

Plantains are from West Africa. They are like bananas, but greener in color. Plantains usually need to be cooked. Ask your grocer if he or she can find plantains for you, or check at a specialty store that carries unusual fruits and vegetables.

4 ripe plantains
1 tablespoon butter
1 tablespoon sugar

Peel and slice the plantains into 1/2 inch circles. Heat the butter and add the plantain slices. Cook for 5 to 8 minutes (until slightly brown). Sprinkle the plantain slices with sugar. Allow the sugar to caramelize slightly and then remove from pan. Serve warm.

BEANS AND RICE

1 cup chopped green onions
1 cup chopped green pepper
1 cup chopped red pepper
2 garlic cloves, crushed
2 cups water
2 tablespoons olive oil
1 can chopped or stewed tomatoes
1 teaspoon vinegar
2 16 oz. cans black beans
1/2 teaspoon oregano
3 cups cooked rice

Sauté the onions, peppers, and garlic in olive oil until tender. Stir in the tomatoes and then add the vinegar, beans, seasonings, and a little water. Simmer until heated and serve over hot rice.

Kwaheri!

Kwanzaa is a happy time when African Americans celebrate being together with family and friends. You can do a lot both to celebrate African heritage and to understand and live the Nguzo Saba. Share what you have learned with your parents, your sisters and brothers, and your friends.

Kwanzaa is a time to do all this and more. Celebrate! Wear the African colors of black, red, and green. Most important of all, take time to learn about the past, think about the present, and plan for the future. "Good-bye," or *"Kwaheri!"*

Glossary

activist (AK-tih-vist)
An activist is a person who speaks out for what he or she believes is right in an effort to bring about change. Dr. Karenga is an activist.

ancestors (AN-ses-terz)
Ancestors are family members who came before you. Great-great grandparents are a person's ancestors, for example.

commit (kuh-MIT)
If people commit to something, they promise to work at or involve themselves in it. People who celebrate Kwanzaa commit themselves to the Seven Principles.

commitment (kuh-MIT-ment)
A commitment is an agreement or a promise to do something. Kwanzaa reinforces the commitment to the Seven Principles.

culture (KUL-chur)
Culture is the customs, arts, language, tools, and history of a people. Kwanzaa celebrates African culture.

customs (KUS-tumz)
Customs are habits or practices that are common to a group of people. People from all the African countries have different customs.

harvest (HAR-vest)
The harvest is a time when people gather and pick crops that are ready to use. Kwanzaa is based on African winter harvest celebrations.

heritage (HAIR-ih-tij)
Heritage is what is passed down from one generation to the next. A person's heritage includes customs, culture, and traditions from his or her ancestors.

libation (ly-BAY-shun)
A libation is a ritual that symbolizes respect for one's ancestors. To perform a libation, a wooden cup is filled with a liquid and then tilted so that some of the liquid is poured onto the ground.

meditation (med-ih-TAY-shun)
Meditation is quiet thought about serious things. The last day of Kwanzaa is the Day of Meditation, and people think about their lives, families, communities, and cultures.

principles (PRIN-sih-pulz)
Principles are rules of behavior. Kwanzaa gives African Americans principles by which to live.

reassessment (ree-uh-SESS-ment)
A reassessment is when somebody takes time to rethink something. During Kwanzaa, people reassess what they accomplished during the year.

recommitment (ree-kuh-MIT-ment)
A recommitment is to an agreement or promise to do something another time. During Kwanzaa, people make a recommitment to the Seven Principles.

rituals (RIH-choo-ulz)
Rituals are solemn ceremonies. Lighting the candles of the kinara during Kwanzaa is a ritual.

sauté (saw-TAY)
To sauté means to lightly fry something in oil or butter. A recipe might instruct cooks to sauté vegetables in oil.

spirituals (SPEER-ih-choolz)
Spirituals are emotional songs about God. Spirituals originally were sung by slaves in the United States.

Swahili (swah-HEE-lee)
Swahili is a language spoken in East Africa. The words for the rituals and symbols of Kwanzaa are from Swahili.

African Glossary

Asante. (a-SAHN-tah)
Thank you.

buba (BOO-bah)
A long, colorful, loose garment worn by men

Habari gani? (hah-BAR-ee GAH-nee)
What's the news? What's happening?

Imani (ee-MAH-nee)
One of the Nguzo Saba (Seven Principles): faith

kanga (KAHN-gah)
A loose-fitting garment worn by women

karamu (kah-RAH-moo)
The feast during Kwanzaa held on December 31

kente (KEN-teh)
A cloth made with an African design

kikombe cha umoja (kee-KOM-bay chah oo-MOE-jah)
One of the symbols of Kwanzaa; the cup for libations

kinara (kee-NAH-rah)
One of the symbols of Kwanzaa; a candle holder that represents people's ancestors

kuchunguza tena na kutoa ahadi tena (koo-choon-GOO-zah TAY-nah nah koo-TOE-ah ah-HAH-dee-TAY-nah)
A speech during Kwanzaa that discusses reassessment and recommitment

Kujichagulia (koo-gee-chah-goo-LEE-ah)
One of the Nguzo Saba (Seven Principles): self-determination

kukaribisha (koo-kah-ree-BEE-shah)
A word of welcoming during Kwanzaa

Kuumba (koo-OOM-bah)
One of the Nguzo Saba (Seven Principles): creativity

Kwaheri. (kwah-HAIR-ee)
Good-bye.

matunda ya kwanzaa (ma-TOON-dah yah KWAHN-zah)
First fruits

mazao (mah-ZAH-oh)
One of the symbols of Kwanzaa; fruits and vegetables used to symbolize crops

mishumaa saba (mee-shoo-MAH-ah SAH-bah)
One of the symbols of Kwanzaa; the seven candles (one black, three red, and three green) that symbolize the Nguzo Saba, the Seven Principles

mkeka (mm-KAY-kah)
One of the symbols of Kwanzaa; a place mat of straw that symbolizes the history and traditions of African culture

muhindi (moo-HEEN-dee)
One of the symbols of Kwanzaa; an ear of corn representing children

Nguzo Saba (en-GOO-zoh sah-BAH)
The Seven Principles of Kwanzaa: Umoja, Kujichagulia, Ujima, Ujamaa, Nia, Kuumba, Imani.

Nia (nee-AH)
One of the Nguzo Saba (Seven Principles): purpose

tutaonang (too-tah-oh-NAH-nah)
We will see each other

Ujamaa (oo-jah-MAH-ah)
One of the Nguzo Saba (Seven Principles): cooperative economics (sharing)

Ujima (oo-JEE-mah)
One of the Nguzo Saba (Seven Principles): collective work (working together) and responsibility

Umoja (oo-MOE-jah)
One of the Nguzo Saba (Seven Principles): unity

zawadi (za-WAH-dee)
Gifts given during Kwanzaa

Index

Further Information

Books

Feelings, Muriel. *Jambo Means Hello, and Moja Means One.* New York: Dial Books for Young Readers, 1974.

Goss, Linda, and Marian Barnes. *Talk That Talk: An Anthology of African-American Storytelling.* New York: Touchstone Books, 1989.

The Heritage Library of African Peoples. (A series of books detailing life in various regions and countries of the African continent.) New York: Rosen Publishing.

Karenga, Maulana. *Kwanzaa: A Celebration of Family, Community and Culture.* Los Angeles: University of Sankore Press, 1998.

Murray, Jocelyn. *Africa* (Cultural Atlas for Young People series). New York: Checkmark Books, 1990.

Musgrove, Margaret. *Ashanti to Zulu.* New York: Dial Press, 1976.

Robinson, Edward, and Harriet Robinson. *Twas the Night Before Kwanzaa.* Philadelphia: Black Rhapsody, 1981.

Web Sites

Visit Dr. Karenga's official Kwanzaa Web site:
http://www.officialkwanzaawebsite.org

Read about one family's special Kwanzaa celebration:
http://www.agirlsworld.com/amy/pajama/winter/Kwanzaa.html

Look up more recipes for Kwanzaa:
http://members.aol.com/lindano/Course/pages/kwrecipe.html

Learn more about Kwanzaa and find out where you can buy products to celebrate the holiday:
http://www.fortunecity.com/victorian/verona/514/15c.html
http://www.tike.com/celeb-kw.htm